Copyright © 2024 Critmaker.com
All rights reserved.

No portion of this book may be reproduced in any form without written permission from the publisher or author.

This publication is designed to provide accurate and authoritative information in regard to the subject matter covered. It is sold with the understanding that neither the author nor the publisher is engaged in rendering safety or manufacturing services. While the publisher and author have used their best efforts in preparing this book, they make no representations or warranties with respect to the accuracy or completeness of the contents of this book and specifically disclaim any implied warranties of merchantability or fitness for a particular purpose. No warranty may be created or extended by sales representatives or written sales materials. The advice and strategies contained herein may not be suitable for your situation. You should consult with a professional when appropriate. Neither the publisher nor the author shall be liable for any loss of profit or any other commercial damages, including but not limited to special, incidental, consequential, personal, or other damages. All trademarks, service marks, and company names are the property of their respective owners.

1st Edition 2024

ABOUT CRITMAKER

Critmaker.com is an online store, label and publisher. We specialise in education, supplies for dice and mould-making, dice-making kits, apparel and merchandise.

WE'RE NOT THE CRITMAKER, _YOU ARE!_

A Critmaker is someone who's passionate about dice craft, and bringing new handmade creations into the world. A Critmaker is someone who wields the hand of fate and whose creations change any mundane encounter into an adventure!

Our only goal is to see more dice fans become makers, and to make the learning curve as easy as possible to help grow the community.

To the dice makers reading this: I am in awe of the incredible, creative images that fill my social feeds. You are the real heroes, the real Critmakers! Our only job is to support your passion.

If we can do anything to make your lives easier or inspire new and upcoming dice makers, we're here to help.

CRITMAKER.COM

INTRODUCTION

While this journal is a companion to The Critmaker™ Guide to Dice Craft, there's no assumed knowledge – in fact, there's nothing in here about making dice at all! The journal asks you to look within for each set of dice to understand your inspiration and think about your desired outcomes. It's both a way of keeping track of your designs for future use *and* a way to measure your progress as a dice maker.

This is not about perfection! Resin and making dice is messy! Allow these pages to be filled with experimentation, imperfect ideas and unexpected successes.

At the start, you'll find an index for you to add the title and page number of your designs. This is an easy way to reference the entries in your journal. After every 10th design, there's a page to remind you to reflect back on your designs and ask three simple questions.

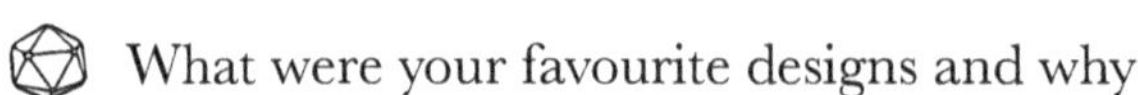 What were your favourite designs and why?

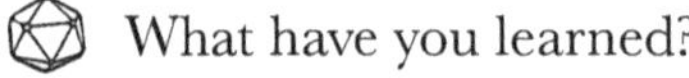 What have you learned?

What do you think you need to improve?

As you continue your journey and continue this exercise, you'll be amazed at how quickly you progress!

I hope this journal helps you to grow as a dice-maker, as it has me.

Thanks for coming along on this journey!

Aaron!

USING THE GUIDE

While it's fun to just jump in and start pouring dice, it's better to go in with a plan or some inspiration. Take a minute before mixing your resin and decide what you hope to achieve.

Each journal page has the following sections:

INSPIRATION

Many things can inspire you: a scene in a movie, a painting, a favourite game or your character in D&D. If the dice are a gift, what does the recipient love? Write down the inspiration, even if you don't directly reference it in the materials!

PALETTE

What colours reflect the inspiration? Is it a night sky or a misty forest? Write down the colours that come to mind or colour them in the d20 at the bottom if that helps.

MIX-INS

Mix-ins are anything you add to your resin, such as mica powders, alcohol inks, glitters, foils, etc.

RESIN

Different resins have different properties, it's good to mention which one you used in case you switch brands and can't get the effect you wanted.

REST

This is how long you waited after mixing to pour your dice. Many techniques require you to wait until the resin has a honey consistency. Depending on the working time of your resin, this may take more or less time and different consistencies have different effects.

TECHNIQUE

There are a huge number of techniques and we go over the most popular ones in our guide. If you're planning a dirty pour, a petri or maybe even a liquid core dice, take note of the technique you used.

POURING & MIXING DETAILS

The most important part of any experiment is the notes! How did you mix the resin, did you use a split-pour cup, did you layer the black on the gold or the gold on the black?

Try something like *"I mixed two scoops of blue mica powder into the resin and then added 2 drops of blue ink, followed by 2 drops of black and three drops of gold."* – Be as detailed as possible for your future self!

NOTES

The last note section is for finishing, polishing or learning, write whatever you think will help you the most.

D20

For visual people, the D20 at the bottom of the page is a place for you to colour, sketch or paint your idea!

DESIGN *Forest Morning Light*   **DATE** *01/01/2024*

INSPIRATION

My character, Dhara, has fond memories of walking through the forest in the early morning light. The sun shines through the trees like gold, bathing the trails in beautiful light.

PALETTE

Jade green with lots of gold shining through. I want the gold to catch the light.

MIX-INS

Green mica powder and LOTS of gold foil — and a faint hint of glitter!

TECHNIQUE   Basic Pour

METHOD   RESIN *Barnes EpoxyCast*   REST __40__ MINS

POURING & MIXING DETAILS

I added a single scoop of mica powder and stirred thoroughly. After that I mixed in two large scoops of gold foil followed by a few drops of iridescent glitter ink.

NOTES

I had a tiny void on one face (fixable). I LOVE how these turned out! Next time I'd add less gold foil and more gold glitter instead.

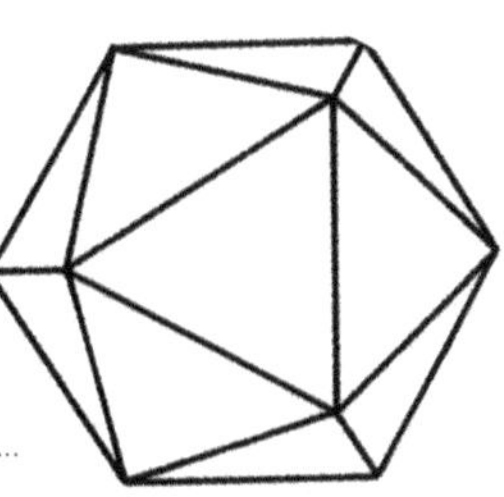

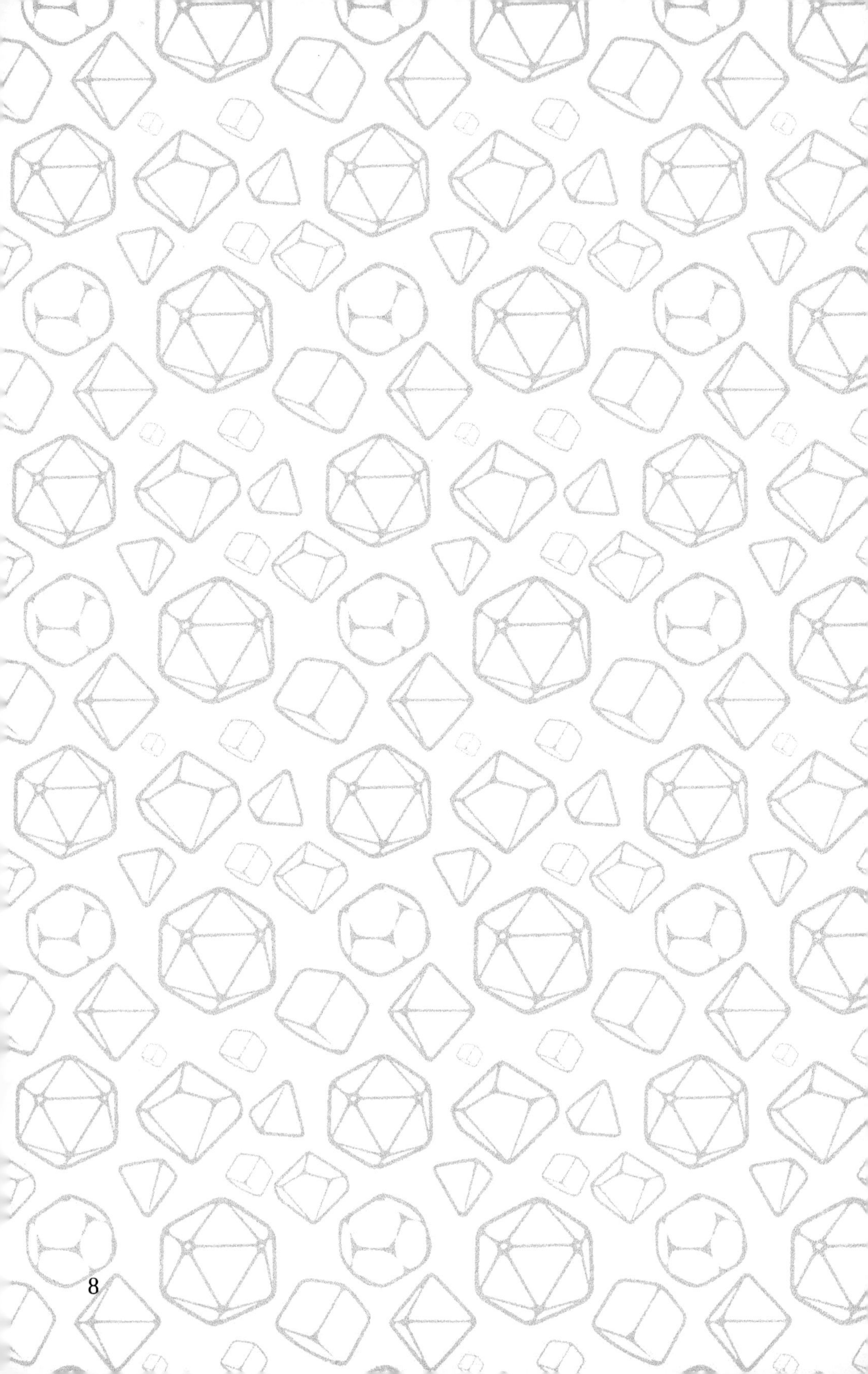

"CREATIVITY IS ALLOWING YOURSELF
TO MAKE MISTAKES. ART IS KNOWING
WHICH ONES TO KEEP."

- SCOTT ADAMS

DESIGN INDEX

DESIGN	PAGE	DESIGN	PAGE

Design Index

Design	Page

Design	Page

INSPIRATION

....
....
....
....

PALETTE   MIX-INS

....
....
....

TECHNIQUE ....

METHOD   RESIN .... REST .... MINS

POURING & MIXING DETAILS

....
....
....
....

NOTES

....
....
....

INSPIRATION

....

....

....

....

PALETTE   MIX-INS

....

....

....

TECHNIQUE ....

METHOD   RESIN ....   REST .... MINS

POURING & MIXING DETAILS

....

....

....

....

NOTES

....

....

....

INSPIRATION

....

....

....

....

PALETTE

....

....

....

MIX-INS

TECHNIQUE ....

METHOD

RESIN .... REST .... MINS

POURING & MIXING DETAILS

....

....

....

NOTES

....

....

....

Design .... Date ....

Inspiration

....

....

....

....

Palette   Mix-Ins

....

....

....

Technique ....

Method   Resin ....   Rest .... Mins

Pouring & Mixing Details

....

....

....

....

Notes

....

....

....

DESIGN .... DATE..

INSPIRATION

....
....
....
....

PALETTE   MIX-INS

....
....
....

TECHNIQUE ....

METHOD   RESIN .... REST .... MINS

POURING & MIXING DETAILS

....
....
....
....

NOTES

....
....
....

INSPIRATION

....

....

....

....

PALETTE   MIX-INS

....

....

....

TECHNIQUE ....

METHOD   RESIN .... REST .... MINS

POURING & MIXING DETAILS

....

....

....

....

NOTES

....

....

....

Inspiration

....
....
....
....

Palette   Mix-Ins

....
....
....

Technique ....

Method   Resin .... Rest .... Mins

Pouring & Mixing Details

....
....
....

Notes

....
....
....

Design ...... Date ......

Inspiration

Palette

Mix-Ins

Technique ......

Method   Resin ...... Rest ...... Mins

Pouring & Mixing Details

Notes

INSPIRATION

....

....

....

....

PALETTE   MIX-INS

....

....

....

TECHNIQUE   ....

METHOD   RESIN .... REST .... MINS

POURING & MIXING DETAILS

....

....

....

....

NOTES

....

....

....

INSPIRATION

PALETTE

MIX-INS

TECHNIQUE ....

METHOD

RESIN .... REST .... MINS

POURING & MIXING DETAILS

NOTES

Design Reflection

24

Favourite Designs

Lessons Learned

Improvements To Make

Notes

DESIGN .... DATE ....

INSPIRATION

....
....
....
....

PALETTE   MIX-INS

....
....
....

TECHNIQUE ....

METHOD   RESIN .... REST .... MINS

POURING & MIXING DETAILS

....
....
....
....

NOTES

....
....
....

INSPIRATION

PALETTE

MIX-INS

TECHNIQUE ....

METHOD

RESIN .... REST .... MINS

POURING & MIXING DETAILS

NOTES

INSPIRATION

....

....

....

....

PALETTE   MIX-INS

....

....

....

TECHNIQUE ....

METHOD   RESIN .... REST .... MINS

POURING & MIXING DETAILS

....

....

....

....

NOTES

....

....

....

Design .... Date ....

Inspiration

....

....

....

....

Palette   Mix-Ins

....

....

....

Technique ....

Method   Resin .... Rest .... Mins

Pouring & Mixing Details

....

....

....

....

Notes

....

....

....

INSPIRATION

PALETTE

MIX-INS

TECHNIQUE

METHOD

RESIN .... REST .... MINS

POURING & MIXING DETAILS

NOTES

INSPIRATION

....

....

....

PALETTE

....

....

....

MIX-INS

....

....

....

TECHNIQUE ....

METHOD   RESIN ....   REST .... MINS

POURING & MIXING DETAILS

....

....

....

NOTES

....

....

....

INSPIRATION

....

....

....

....

PALETTE

....

....

....

MIX-INS

....

....

....

TECHNIQUE ....

METHOD   RESIN .... REST .... MINS

POURING & MIXING DETAILS

....

....

....

....

NOTES

....

....

....

Design .... Date ....

Inspiration

....

....

....

....

Palette   Mix-Ins

....

....

....

Technique ....

Method

Resin .... Rest .... Mins

Pouring & Mixing Details

....

....

....

....

Notes

....

....

....

Inspiration

....
....
....
....

Palette

....
....
....

Mix-Ins

....
....
....

Technique ....

Method Resin .... Rest .... Mins

Pouring & Mixing Details

....
....
....
....

Notes

....
....
....

INSPIRATION

PALETTE   MIX-INS

TECHNIQUE ....

METHOD   RESIN .... REST .... MINS

POURING & MIXING DETAILS

NOTES

DESIGN REFLECTION

Favourite Designs

Lessons Learned

Improvements To Make

Notes

Inspiration

....
....
....
....

Palette   Mix-Ins

....
....
....

Technique ....

Method   Resin .... Rest .... Mins

Pouring & Mixing Details

....
....
....
....

Notes

....
....
....

INSPIRATION

....

....

....

....

PALETTE   MIX-INS

....

....

....

TECHNIQUE ....

METHOD   RESIN ....   REST .... MINS

POURING & MIXING DETAILS

....

....

....

....

NOTES

....

....

....

Inspiration

....

....

....

....

Palette

Mix-Ins

....

....

....

Technique ....

Method   Resin .... Rest .... Mins

Pouring & Mixing Details

....

....

....

....

Notes

....

....

....

INSPIRATION

PALETTE   MIX-INS

TECHNIQUE ....

METHOD   RESIN ....   REST .... MINS

POURING & MIXING DETAILS

NOTES

Inspiration

....
....
....
....

Palette   Mix-Ins

....
....
....

Technique ....

Method   Resin .... Rest .... Mins

Pouring & Mixing Details

....
....
....
....

Notes

....
....
....

Inspiration

....

....

....

....

Palette

Mix-Ins

....

....

....

Technique ....

Method   Resin ....   Rest .... Mins

Pouring & Mixing Details

....

....

....

....

Notes

....

....

....

Inspiration

....

....

....

....

Palette

....

....

....

Mix-Ins

....

....

....

Technique ....

Method   Resin ....   Rest .... Mins

Pouring & Mixing Details

....

....

....

....

Notes

....

....

....

INSPIRATION

....
....
....
....

PALETTE   MIX-INS

....
....
....

TECHNIQUE ....

METHOD   RESIN ....   REST .... MINS

POURING & MIXING DETAILS

....
....
....
....

NOTES

....
....
....

DESIGN .... DATE ....

INSPIRATION

....

....

....

....

PALETTE   MIX-INS

....

....

....

TECHNIQUE ....

METHOD   RESIN .... REST .... MINS

POURING & MIXING DETAILS

....

....

....

....

NOTES

....

....

....

DESIGN .... DATE ....

INSPIRATION

....
....
....
....

PALETTE   MIX-INS

....
....
....

TECHNIQUE ....

METHOD   RESIN .... REST .... MINS

POURING & MIXING DETAILS

....
....
....
....

NOTES

....
....
....

Design Reflection

Favourite Designs

Lessons Learned

Improvements To Make

NOTES

Design .... Date ....

INSPIRATION

....

....

....

....

Palette   Mix-Ins

....

....

....

Technique ....

METHOD   Resin ....   Rest .... Mins

Pouring & Mixing Details

....

....

....

....

NOTES

....

....

....

INSPIRATION

....
....
....
....

PALETTE   MIX-INS

....
....
....

TECHNIQUE ....

METHOD   RESIN ....   REST .... MINS

POURING & MIXING DETAILS

....
....
....
....

NOTES

....
....
....

INSPIRATION

PALETTE

MIX-INS

TECHNIQUE

METHOD

RESIN .... REST .... MINS

POURING & MIXING DETAILS

NOTES

DESIGN .... DATE ....

INSPIRATION

....

....

....

....

PALETTE   MIX-INS

....

....

....

TECHNIQUE ....

METHOD   RESIN .... REST .... MINS

POURING & MIXING DETAILS

....

....

....

....

NOTES

....

....

....

INSPIRATION

....

....

....

....

PALETTE   MIX-INS

....

....

....

TECHNIQUE ....

METHOD   RESIN .... REST .... MINS

POURING & MIXING DETAILS

....

....

....

....

NOTES

....

....

....

INSPIRATION

....
....
....
....

PALETTE   MIX-INS

....
....
....

TECHNIQUE ....

METHOD   RESIN ....   REST .... MINS

POURING & MIXING DETAILS

....
....
....
....

NOTES

....
....
....

DESIGN .... DATE ....

INSPIRATION

....
....
....
....

PALETTE   MIX-INS

....
....
....

TECHNIQUE ....

METHOD   RESIN .... REST .... MINS

POURING & MIXING DETAILS

....
....
....
....

NOTES

....
....

INSPIRATION

PALETTE

MIX-INS

TECHNIQUE

METHOD

RESIN .... REST .... MINS

POURING & MIXING DETAILS

NOTES

DESIGN .... DATE ....

INSPIRATION

....

....

....

....

PALETTE   MIX-INS

....

....

....

TECHNIQUE ....

METHOD   RESIN .... REST .... MINS

POURING & MIXING DETAILS

....

....

....

....

NOTES

....

....

....

INSPIRATION

....
....
....

PALETTE   MIX-INS

....
....
....

TECHNIQUE ....

METHOD   RESIN ....   REST .... MINS

POURING & MIXING DETAILS

....
....
....

NOTES

....
....

Design Reflection

Favourite Designs

Lessons Learned

Improvements To Make

NOTES

Inspiration

....
....
....
....

Palette   Mix-Ins

....
....
....

Technique ....

Method   Resin .... Rest .... Mins

Pouring & Mixing Details

....
....
....
....

Notes

....
....
....

Inspiration

....

....

....

....

Palette

Mix-Ins

....

....

....

Technique ....

Method   Resin ....   Rest .... Mins

Pouring & Mixing Details

....

....

....

Notes

....

....

....

Design .... Date ....

Inspiration

....
....
....
....

Palette

....
....
....

Mix-Ins

....
....
....

Technique ....

Method

Resin .... Rest .... Mins

Pouring & Mixing Details

....
....
....
....

Notes

....
....
....

DESIGN .... DATE ....

INSPIRATION

....
....
....
....

PALETTE   MIX-INS

....
....
....

TECHNIQUE ....

METHOD   RESIN .... REST .... MINS

POURING & MIXING DETAILS

....
....
....
....

NOTES

....
....
....

DESIGN ...... DATE......

INSPIRATION

PALETTE

MIX-INS

TECHNIQUE ......

METHOD   RESIN ...... REST ...... MINS

POURING & MIXING DETAILS

NOTES

INSPIRATION

PALETTE

MIX-INS

TECHNIQUE

METHOD

RESIN .... REST .... MINS

POURING & MIXING DETAILS

NOTES

Inspiration

....

....

....

....

Palette   Mix-Ins

....

....

....

Technique ....

Method   Resin .... Rest .... Mins

Pouring & Mixing Details

....

....

....

....

Notes

....

....

....

DESIGN .... DATE ....

INSPIRATION

....

....

....

....

PALETTE   MIX-INS

....

....

....

TECHNIQUE ....

METHOD   RESIN ....   REST .... MINS

POURING & MIXING DETAILS

....

....

....

....

NOTES

....

....

....

Design .... Date.....................................

Inspiration

....
....
....
....

Palette   Mix-Ins

....
....
....

Technique ....

Method   Resin .... Rest .... Mins

Pouring & Mixing Details

....
....
....
....

Notes

....
....
....

INSPIRATION

....

....

....

....

PALETTE   MIX-INS

....

....

....

TECHNIQUE ....

METHOD   RESIN .... REST .... MINS

POURING & MIXING DETAILS

....

....

....

....

NOTES

....

....

....

DESIGN REFLECTION

72

Favourite Designs

Lessons Learned

Improvements To Make

NOTES

Inspiration

....

....

....

....

Palette   Mix-Ins

....

....

....

Technique   ....

Method   Resin .... Rest .... Mins

Pouring & Mixing Details

....

....

....

....

Notes

....

....

....

INSPIRATION

PALETTE

MIX-INS

TECHNIQUE

METHOD

RESIN .... REST .... MINS

POURING & MIXING DETAILS

NOTES

INSPIRATION

....
....
....
....

PALETTE   MIX-INS

....
....
....

TECHNIQUE ....

METHOD   RESIN .... REST .... MINS

POURING & MIXING DETAILS

....
....
....
....

NOTES

....
....
....

DESIGN .... DATE ....

INSPIRATION

....
....
....
....

PALETTE

MIX-INS

....
....
....

TECHNIQUE ....

METHOD   RESIN .... REST .... MINS

POURING & MIXING DETAILS

....
....
....
....

NOTES

....
....
....

Design .... Date ....

Inspiration

....

....

....

....

Palette   Mix-Ins

....

....

....

Technique ....

Method   Resin .... Rest .... Mins

Pouring & Mixing Details

....

....

....

....

Notes

....

....

....

Inspiration

....
....
....

Palette

Mix-Ins

....
....
....

Technique ....

Method   Resin .... Rest .... Mins

Pouring & Mixing Details

....
....
....
....

Notes

....
....
....

DESIGN .... DATE ....

INSPIRATION

....
....
....
....

PALETTE   MIX-INS

....
....
....

TECHNIQUE ....

METHOD   RESIN .... REST .... MINS

POURING & MIXING DETAILS

....
....
....
....

NOTES

....
....
....

INSPIRATION

....

....

....

....

PALETTE

MIX-INS

....

....

....

....

....

TECHNIQUE ....

METHOD   RESIN .... REST .... MINS

POURING & MIXING DETAILS

....

....

....

....

NOTES

....

....

....

Inspiration

....
....
....
....

Palette

Mix-Ins

....
....
....

....
....
....

Technique ....

Method   Resin .... Rest .... Mins

Pouring & Mixing Details

....
....
....
....

Notes

....
....
....

INSPIRATION

PALETTE

MIX-INS

TECHNIQUE

METHOD   RESIN .... REST .... MINS

POURING & MIXING DETAILS

NOTES

Design Reflection

84

Favourite Designs

Lessons Learned

Improvements To Make

Notes

Design .... Date...

Inspiration

....
....
....
....

Palette

Mix-Ins

....

....

....

Technique ....

Method

Resin .... Rest .... Mins

Pouring & Mixing Details

....
....
....
....

Notes

....
....
....

INSPIRATION

....

....

....

PALETTE

....

....

....

MIX-INS

....

....

....

TECHNIQUE ....

METHOD

RESIN .... REST .... MINS

POURING & MIXING DETAILS

....

....

....

....

NOTES

....

....

....

Inspiration

....
....
....
....

Palette

....
....
....

Mix-Ins

....
....

Technique ....

Method

Resin .... Rest .... Mins

Pouring & Mixing Details

....
....
....
....

Notes

....
....
....

Inspiration

Palette

Mix-Ins

Technique

Method   Resin .... Rest .... Mins

Pouring & Mixing Details

Notes

INSPIRATION

....

....

....

....

PALETTE

MIX-INS

....

....

....

TECHNIQUE ....

METHOD   RESIN .... REST .... MINS

POURING & MIXING DETAILS

....

....

....

....

NOTES

....

....

....

Inspiration

....
....
....
....

Palette   Mix-Ins

....
....
....

Technique ....

Method   Resin .... Rest .... Mins

Pouring & Mixing Details

....
....
....
....

Notes

....
....
....

Inspiration

....

....

....

....

Palette

Mix-Ins

....

....

....

....

....

....

Technique ....

Method Resin .... Rest .... Mins

Pouring & Mixing Details

....

....

....

....

Notes

....

....

....

INSPIRATION

PALETTE

MIX-INS

TECHNIQUE ....

METHOD   RESIN ....   REST .... MINS

POURING & MIXING DETAILS

NOTES

INSPIRATION

PALETTE

MIX-INS

TECHNIQUE

METHOD

RESIN .... REST .... MINS

POURING & MIXING DETAILS

NOTES

DESIGN .... DATE ....

INSPIRATION

....
....
....
....

PALETTE

MIX-INS

....
....
....

TECHNIQUE ....

METHOD

RESIN .... REST .... MINS

POURING & MIXING DETAILS

....
....
....
....

NOTES

....
....
....

Design Reflection

Favourite Designs

Lessons Learned

Improvements To Make

NOTES

Inspiration

....

....

....

....

Palette

Mix-Ins

....

....

....

Technique ....

Method

Resin .... Rest .... Mins

Pouring & Mixing Details

....

....

....

....

Notes

....

....

DESIGN .... DATE ....

INSPIRATION

....
....
....
....

PALETTE   MIX-INS

....
....
....

TECHNIQUE ....

METHOD   RESIN .... REST .... MINS

POURING & MIXING DETAILS

....
....
....
....

NOTES

....
....
....

INSPIRATION

....

....

....

....

PALETTE   MIX-INS

....

....

....

TECHNIQUE ....

METHOD   RESIN .... REST .... MINS

POURING & MIXING DETAILS

....

....

....

....

NOTES

....

....

....

INSPIRATION

....
....
....
....

PALETTE   MIX-INS

....
....
....

TECHNIQUE ....

METHOD   RESIN .... REST .... MINS

POURING & MIXING DETAILS

....
....
....
....

NOTES

....
....
....

DESIGN .... DATE ....

INSPIRATION

....
....
....
....

PALETTE   MIX-INS

....
....
....

TECHNIQUE ....

METHOD   RESIN .... REST .... MINS

POURING & MIXING DETAILS

....
....
....
....

NOTES

....
....
....

INSPIRATION

....

....

....

....

PALETTE

MIX-INS

TECHNIQUE ....

METHOD   RESIN ....   REST .... MINS

POURING & MIXING DETAILS

....

....

....

....

NOTES

....

....

Design .... Date ....

Inspiration

....
....
....
....

Palette

....
....
....

Mix-Ins

....
....
....

Technique ....

Method

Resin .... Rest .... Mins

Pouring & Mixing Details

....
....
....
....

Notes

....
....
....

INSPIRATION

....
....
....
....

PALETTE | MIX-INS
....
....
....

TECHNIQUE ....

METHOD   RESIN .... REST .... MINS

POURING & MIXING DETAILS

....
....
....
....

NOTES

....
....
....

INSPIRATION

....
....
....
....

PALETTE   MIX-INS

....
....
....

TECHNIQUE   ....

METHOD   RESIN .... REST .... MINS

POURING & MIXING DETAILS

....
....
....

NOTES

....
....
....

DESIGN .... DATE ....

INSPIRATION

....
....
....
....

PALETTE   MIX-INS

....
....
....

TECHNIQUE ....

METHOD   RESIN ....   REST .... MINS

POURING & MIXING DETAILS

....
....
....
....

NOTES

....
....
....

Design Reflection

Favourite Designs

Lessons Learned

Improvements To Make

NOTES

INSPIRATION

....

....

....

....

PALETTE   MIX-INS

....

....

....

TECHNIQUE ....

METHOD   RESIN .... REST .... MINS

POURING & MIXING DETAILS

....

....

....

....

NOTES

....

....

....

INSPIRATION

PALETTE

MIX-INS

TECHNIQUE

METHOD   RESIN .... REST .... MINS

POURING & MIXING DETAILS

NOTES

Inspiration

....

....

....

....

Palette   Mix-Ins

....

....

....

Technique ....

Method   Resin .... Rest .... Mins

Pouring & Mixing Details

....

....

....

....

Notes

....

....

....

Design .... Date ....

Inspiration

....

....

....

....

Palette

....

....

....

Mix-Ins

....

....

....

Technique ....

Method   Resin ....   Rest .... Mins

Pouring & Mixing Details

....

....

....

....

Notes

....

....

....

Inspiration

....

....

....

....

Palette

Mix-Ins

....

....

....

Technique ....

Method   Resin .... Rest .... Mins

Pouring & Mixing Details

....

....

....

....

Notes

....

....

....

Inspiration

....
....
....

Palette   Mix-Ins

....
....
....

Technique ....

Method   Resin .... Rest .... Mins

Pouring & Mixing Details

....
....
....

Notes

....
....
....

INSPIRATION

....

....

....

....

PALETTE   MIX-INS

....

....

....

TECHNIQUE ....

METHOD   RESIN .... REST .... MINS

POURING & MIXING DETAILS

....

....

....

....

NOTES

....

....

....

INSPIRATION

PALETTE

MIX-INS

TECHNIQUE ....

METHOD

RESIN .... REST .... MINS

POURING & MIXING DETAILS

NOTES

INSPIRATION

....

....

....

....

PALETTE   MIX-INS

....

....

....

TECHNIQUE ....

METHOD   RESIN .... REST .... MINS

POURING & MIXING DETAILS

....

....

....

....

NOTES

....

....

....

DESIGN .... DATE ....

INSPIRATION

....
....
....
....

PALETTE   MIX-INS

....
....
....

TECHNIQUE ....

METHOD   RESIN .... REST .... MINS

POURING & MIXING DETAILS

....
....
....
....

NOTES

....
....
....

Design Reflection

Favourite Designs

Lessons Learned

Improvements To Make

Notes

Inspiration

....

....

....

....

Palette   Mix-Ins

....

....

....

Technique ....

Method   Resin .... Rest .... Mins

Pouring & Mixing Details

....

....

....

....

Notes

....

....

....

Inspiration

....

....

....

....

Palette   Mix-Ins

....

....

....

Technique ....

Method   Resin .... Rest .... Mins

Pouring & Mixing Details

....

....

....

....

Notes

....

....

....

INSPIRATION

....

....

....

....

PALETTE   MIX-INS

....

....

....

TECHNIQUE ....

METHOD   RESIN .... REST .... MINS

POURING & MIXING DETAILS

....

....

....

....

NOTES

....

....

....

DESIGN ...... DATE ......

INSPIRATION

PALETTE

MIX-INS

TECHNIQUE

METHOD   RESIN ...... REST ...... MINS

POURING & MIXING DETAILS

NOTES

INSPIRATION

....

....

....

....

PALETTE   MIX-INS

....

....

....

TECHNIQUE   ....

METHOD   RESIN .... REST .... MINS

POURING & MIXING DETAILS

....

....

....

....

NOTES

....

....

....

INSPIRATION

PALETTE   MIX-INS

TECHNIQUE ....

METHOD   RESIN .... REST .... MINS

POURING & MIXING DETAILS

NOTES

DESIGN .... DATE ....

INSPIRATION

....

....

....

....

PALETTE   MIX-INS

....

....

....

TECHNIQUE ....

METHOD   RESIN .... REST .... MINS

POURING & MIXING DETAILS

....

....

....

....

NOTES

....

....

....

INSPIRATION

....

....

....

....

PALETTE

....

....

....

TECHNIQUE ....

METHOD   RESIN ....   REST .... MINS

POURING & MIXING DETAILS

....

....

....

....

NOTES

....

....

....

MIX-INS

....

....

....

INSPIRATION

....

....

....

PALETTE   MIX-INS

....

....

....

TECHNIQUE   ....

METHOD   RESIN .... REST .... MINS

POURING & MIXING DETAILS

....

....

....

NOTES

....

....

....

Inspiration

....

....

....

Palette   Mix-Ins

....

....

....

Technique ....

Method   Resin .... Rest .... Mins

Pouring & Mixing Details

....

....

....

....

Notes

....

....

....

Design Reflection

Favourite Designs

Lessons Learned

Improvements To Make

NOTES

Inspiration

....

....

....

....

Palette

Mix-Ins

....

....

....

Technique ....

Method
Resin .... Rest .... Mins

Pouring & Mixing Details

....

....

....

....

Notes

....

....

....

DESIGN .... DATE ....

INSPIRATION

....
....
....

PALETTE   MIX-INS

....
....
....

TECHNIQUE ....

METHOD   RESIN .... REST .... MINS

POURING & MIXING DETAILS

....
....
....
....

NOTES

....
....
....

INSPIRATION

....

....

....

....

PALETTE   MIX-INS

....

....

....

TECHNIQUE ....

METHOD   RESIN .... REST .... MINS

POURING & MIXING DETAILS

....

....

....

....

NOTES

....

....

....

INSPIRATION

....

....

....

....

PALETTE   MIX-INS

....

....

....

TECHNIQUE ....

METHOD   RESIN ....   REST .... MINS

POURING & MIXING DETAILS

....

....

....

....

NOTES

....

....

....

Design .... Date ....

Inspiration

....
....
....
....

Palette   Mix-Ins

....
....
....

Technique   ....

Method   Resin .... Rest .... Mins

Pouring & Mixing Details

....
....
....
....

Notes

....
....
....

Design .... Date ....

Inspiration

....
....
....
....

Palette   Mix-Ins

....
....
....

Technique ....

Method   Resin .... Rest .... Mins

Pouring & Mixing Details

....
....
....
....

Notes

....
....
....

INSPIRATION

....
....
....
....

PALETTE   MIX-INS

....
....
....

TECHNIQUE ....

METHOD   RESIN .... REST .... MINS

POURING & MIXING DETAILS

....
....
....
....

NOTES

....
....
....

INSPIRATION

....

....

....

....

PALETTE

MIX-INS

....

....

....

TECHNIQUE ....

METHOD   RESIN ....   REST .... MINS

POURING & MIXING DETAILS

....

....

....

....

NOTES

....

....

....

Design .... Date ....

Inspiration

....
....
....
....

Palette   Mix-Ins

....
....
....

Technique   ....

Method   Resin .... Rest .... Mins

Pouring & Mixing Details

....
....
....
....

Notes

....
....
....

INSPIRATION

PALETTE

MIX-INS

TECHNIQUE

METHOD

RESIN .... REST .... MINS

POURING & MIXING DETAILS

NOTES

Design Reflection

Favourite Designs

Lessons Learned

Improvements To Make

NOTES

MORE FROM CRITMAKER

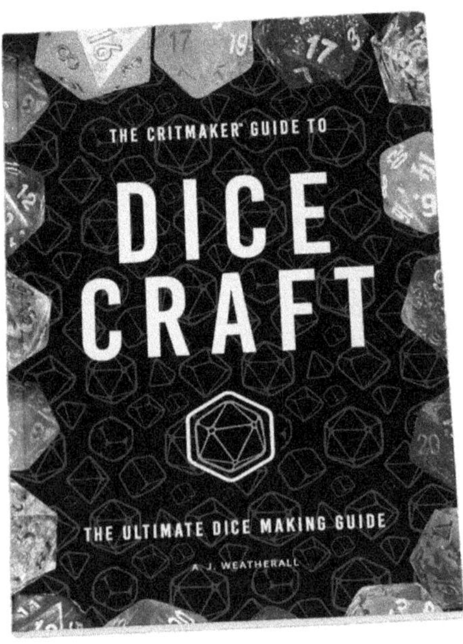

From the halls of the Pharaohs to the plush green velvet of casino tables, dice have played a crucial role in decision making for over 5000 years.

Whether they're made of resin, plastic, glass or even more exotic materials, dice bring the allure of the divine to any game of chance.

As a Critmaker™, you can wield the power of fate. Adventures, quests, and characters will hang in the balance of your creations. Imbued with flashes of color or entire galaxies, your dice will turn any mundane encounter into an adventure.

From simple coloured dice to beautiful "Petri" and "Liquid Core", this guide will teach you everything you need to know to get started in the incredible world of Dice Craft.

GRAB THE ULTIMATE DICE-MAKING GUIDE
FROM AMAZON OR CRITMAKER.COM

www.ingramcontent.com/pod-product-compliance
Lightning Source LLC
Chambersburg PA
CBHW050003040726
47599CB00014B/1189